The Truth About
Santa

There's a Definite Connection Between the Two.

Santa and **Jesus** . . .

Do You Know What They Do?

Mary Kay Worth

To Landon

Mary Kay Worth 11-7-15

AuthorHouse™
1663 Liberty Drive
Bloomington, IN 47403
www.authorhouse.com
Phone: 1 (800) 839-8640

Published by AuthorHouse 3/18/2015

ISBN: 978-1-4969-7391-7 (sc)
978-1-4969-7393-1 (hc)
978-1-4969-7392-4 (e)

Library of Congress Control Number: 2015903662

Print information available on the last page.

Any people depicted in stock imagery provided by Thinkstock are models,
and such images are being used for illustrative purposes only.
Certain stock imagery © Thinkstock.

This book is printed on acid-free paper.

authorHOUSE®

FOREWARD

Every holiday season I share this poem I wrote in the summer of 1988 for my sons ~ Nate and Tom ~ who, at the time, were 4 and 6 years old.

That year was especially difficult. My marriage had ended. In June my sons and I moved home with my parents while I regrouped. I thought divorce was the worst thing that would happen in 1988.

July came. My mother was diagnosed HIV positive.

During that summer, I worked with severe/profound mentally and physically disabled youth. I hand wrote this poem while on breaks there.

I wanted something to give to my boys that would make sense in their young minds about the real story of Christmas and the ever-growing secular trappings of the holiday season. I was trying to make sense of so many things and went to my faith for hope and inspiration in a dark and uncertain time.

This poem did just that. I share it again, adding photos from our decorated homes over the years.

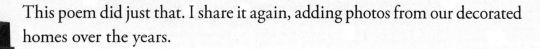

The Santa you know and I know, too,
has a very important job to do.

Santa doesn't just bring presents for all.

He isn't the reason that we "Deck the Hall."

Santa's purpose is bigger, indeed, and has
much to do with souls in need.

Santa doesn't come on Thanksgiving or Halloween.

He doesn't come on days in between.

He always appears on the eve that the Babe
was born in a manger so far away.

Yes, there's a definite connection between the two.
Santa and Jesus. . . do you know what they do?

Jesus lived and died for all of our sin.

He rose from the grave so sinners can win.

Santa's connection is one that makes way
for the big birthday party on Christmas Day!

The dolls, the drums, the gifts Santa brings. . .

the trees, the cookies, the carols we sing,

They're all for the birthday of Jesus, the One,
who came for us all. . . God's only Son!

And Santa's the guy who helps us to see
How happy life with Jesus can be.

And though the presents are for the Christ that lives,

It pleases Him most when He gives.

He gives in the spirit that seems to say,
"I love you all in your own special way!"

So the next time you see the filled Christmas sleigh,

Remember the truth about Santa and our Lord's birthday!

MERRY CHRISTMAS!

About the Author

Child of God, Grandma, Mother, Daughter, Sister

Teacher, Principal, Superintendent, Professor

Traveler, Storyteller, Photographer, Actor, Musician, and Author

In addition to original text, most often inspired by true stories, the photos in all her books are her own. Technology has added the ability to design and bring a vision to life. Mary Kay's dream includes inspiring educators and students to tell stories, write, illustrate, design, and SHARE!

Mary Kay is also the author of ***HEY ELEPHANT! WHERE ARE YOU?*** and ***Dear Deer***.

CPSIA information can be obtained at www.ICGtesting.com
Printed in the USA
LVOW05s2232300915

456416LV00018B/115/P